ORDER LOG BOOK FOR

$ SMALL BUSINESS $

Name: ....

Business Name: ....

Tel: ....

Mobile: ....

E-mail: ....

D1736470

ORDER FORM

Date: ....

Order#: ....

CUSTOMER DETAILS

Name: ....

Address: ....

Company: ....

Tel. .... **E-mail:** ....

ORDER DETAILS

No	Item(s) Description	QTY.	Price	Total
....	....	....	....	....
....	....	....	....	....
....	....	....	....	....
....	....	....	....	....
....	....	....	....	....
....	....	....	....	....
....	....	....	....	....

SHIPPING DETAILS

Shipping method: ....

....

Tracking#: ....

Date shipped: ....

Subtotal: ....

Shipping cost: ....

Discount: ....

Total: ....

NOTES

....

....

....

ORDER FORM

Date:

Order#:

CUSTOMER DETAILS

Name: ....

Address: ....

Company: ....

Tel. .... **E-mail:** ....

ORDER DETAILS

No	Item(s) Description	QTY.	Price	Total
....	....	....	....	....
....	....	....	....	....
....	....	....	....	....
....	....	....	....	....
....	....	....	....	....
....	....	....	....	....
....	....	....	....	....

SHIPPING DETAILS

Shipping method: ....

....

Tracking#: ....

Date shipped: ....

Subtotal: ....

Shipping cost: ....

Discount: ....

Total: ....

NOTES

....

....

....

ORDER FORM

Date: ....

Order#: ....

CUSTOMER DETAILS

Name: ....

Address: ....

Company: ....

Tel. .... **E-mail:** ....

ORDER DETAILS

No	Item(s) Description	QTY.	Price	Total
....	....	....	....	....
....	....	....	....	....
....	....	....	....	....
....	....	....	....	....
....	....	....	....	....
....	....	....	....	....
....	....	....	....	....

SHIPPING DETAILS

Shipping method: ....

....

Tracking#: ....

Date shipped: ....

Subtotal: ....

Shipping cost: ....

Discount: ....

Total: ....

NOTES

....

....

....

ORDER FORM

Date:

Order#:

CUSTOMER DETAILS

Name: ....

Address: ....

Company: ....

Tel. .... E-mail: ....

ORDER DETAILS

No	Item(s) Description	QTY.	Price	Total
....	....	....	....	....
....	....	....	....	....
....	....	....	....	....
....	....	....	....	....
....	....	....	....	....
....	....	....	....	....
....	....	....	....	....

SHIPPING DETAILS

Shipping method: ....

....

Tracking#: ....

Date shipped: ....

Subtotal: ....

Shipping cost: ....

Discount: ....

Total: ....

NOTES

....

....

....

ORDER FORM

Date:

Order#:

CUSTOMER DETAILS

Name: ....

Address: ....

Company: ....

Tel. .... **E-mail:** ....

ORDER DETAILS

No	Item(s) Description	QTY.	Price	Total
....	....	....	....	....
....	....	....	....	....
....	....	....	....	....
....	....	....	....	....
....	....	....	....	....
....	....	....	....	....
....	....	....	....	....

SHIPPING DETAILS

Shipping method: ....   **Subtotal:** ....

....   **Shipping cost:** ....

Tracking#: ....   **Discount:** ....

Date shipped: ....   **Total:** ....

NOTES

....

....

ORDER FORM

Date:

Order#:

CUSTOMER DETAILS

Name: ....

Address: ....

Company: ....

Tel. .... E-mail: ....

ORDER DETAILS

No	Item(s) Description	QTY.	Price	Total
....	....	....	....	....
....	....	....	....	....
....	....	....	....	....
....	....	....	....	....
....	....	....	....	....
....	....	....	....	....
....	....	....	....	....

SHIPPING DETAILS

Shipping method: ....

....

Tracking#: ....

Date shipped: ....

Subtotal: ....

Shipping cost: ....

Discount: ....

Total: ....

NOTES

....

....

....

ORDER FORM

Date:

Order#:

CUSTOMER DETAILS

Name: ....

Address: ....

Company: ....

Tel. .... **E-mail:** ....

ORDER DETAILS

No	Item(s) Description	QTY.	Price	Total
....	....	....	....	....
....	....	....	....	....
....	....	....	....	....
....	....	....	....	....
....	....	....	....	....
....	....	....	....	....
....	....	....	....	....

SHIPPING DETAILS

Shipping method: ....

....

Tracking#: ....

Date shipped: ....

Subtotal: ....

Shipping cost: ....

Discount: ....

Total: ....

NOTES

....

....

....

ORDER FORM

Date:

Order#:

CUSTOMER DETAILS

Name: ....

Address: ....

Company: ....

Tel. .... E-mail: ....

ORDER DETAILS

No	Item(s) Description	QTY.	Price	Total
....	....	....	....	....
....	....	....	....	....
....	....	....	....	....
....	....	....	....	....
....	....	....	....	....
....	....	....	....	....
....	....	....	....	....

SHIPPING DETAILS

Shipping method: ....

....

Tracking#: ....

Date shipped: ....

Subtotal: ....

Shipping cost: ....

Discount: ....

Total: ....

NOTES

....

....

....

ORDER FORM

Date:

Order#:

CUSTOMER DETAILS

Name: ....

Address: ....

Company: ....

Tel. .... **E-mail:** ....

ORDER DETAILS

No	Item(s) Description	QTY.	Price	Total
....	....	....	....	....
....	....	....	....	....
....	....	....	....	....
....	....	....	....	....
....	....	....	....	....
....	....	....	....	....
....	....	....	....	....

SHIPPING DETAILS

Shipping method: ....

....

Tracking#: ....

Date shipped: ....

Subtotal: ....

Shipping cost: ....

Discount: ....

Total: ....

NOTES

....

....

....

ORDER FORM

Date:

Order#:

CUSTOMER DETAILS

Name: ....

Address: ....

Company: ....

Tel. .... E-mail: ....

ORDER DETAILS

No	Item(s) Description	QTY.	Price	Total
....	....	....	....	....
....	....	....	....	....
....	....	....	....	....
....	....	....	....	....
....	....	....	....	....
....	....	....	....	....
....	....	....	....	....

SHIPPING DETAILS

Shipping method: ....

....

Tracking#: ....

Date shipped: ....

Subtotal: ....

Shipping cost: ....

Discount: ....

Total: ....

NOTES

....

....

....

ORDER FORM

Date:

Order#:

CUSTOMER DETAILS

Name: ....

Address: ....

Company: ....

Tel. .... **E-mail:** ....

ORDER DETAILS

No	Item(s) Description	QTY.	Price	Total
....	....	....	....	....
....	....	....	....	....
....	....	....	....	....
....	....	....	....	....
....	....	....	....	....
....	....	....	....	....
....	....	....	....	....

SHIPPING DETAILS

Shipping method: ....

....

Tracking#: ....

Date shipped: ....

Subtotal: ....

Shipping cost: ....

Discount: ....

Total: ....

NOTES

....

....

....

ORDER FORM

Date:

Order#:

CUSTOMER DETAILS

Name: ....

Address: ....

Company: ....

Tel. .... E-mail: ....

ORDER DETAILS

No	Item(s) Description	QTY.	Price	Total
......	....	....	....	....
......	....	....	....	....
......	....	....	....	....
......	....	....	....	....
......	....	....	....	....
......	....	....	....	....
......	....	....	....	....

SHIPPING DETAILS

Shipping method: ....

....

Tracking#: ....

Date shipped: ....

Subtotal: ....

Shipping cost: ....

Discount: ....

Total: ....

NOTES

....

....

....

ORDER FORM

Date:

Order#:

CUSTOMER DETAILS

Name: ....

Address: ....

Company: ....

Tel. .... **E-mail:** ....

ORDER DETAILS

No	Item(s) Description	QTY.	Price	Total
....	....	....	....	....
....	....	....	....	....
....	....	....	....	....
....	....	....	....	....
....	....	....	....	....
....	....	....	....	....
....	....	....	....	....

SHIPPING DETAILS

Shipping method: ....

....

Tracking#: ....

Date shipped: ....

Subtotal: ....

Shipping cost: ....

Discount: ....

Total: ....

NOTES

....

....

....

ORDER FORM

Date:

Order#:

CUSTOMER DETAILS

Name: ....

Address: ....

Company: ....

Tel. .... E-mail: ....

ORDER DETAILS

No	Item(s) Description	QTY.	Price	Total
....	....	....	....	....
....	....	....	....	....
....	....	....	....	....
....	....	....	....	....
....	....	....	....	....
....	....	....	....	....
....	....	....	....	....

SHIPPING DETAILS

Shipping method: ....

....

Tracking#: ....

Date shipped: ....

Subtotal: ....

Shipping cost: ....

Discount: ....

Total: ....

NOTES

....

....

....

ORDER FORM

Date: ....

Order#: ....

CUSTOMER DETAILS

Name: ....

Address: ....

Company: ....

Tel. .... **E-mail:** ....

ORDER DETAILS

No	Item(s) Description	QTY.	Price	Total
....	....	....	....	....
....	....	....	....	....
....	....	....	....	....
....	....	....	....	....
....	....	....	....	....
....	....	....	....	....
....	....	....	....	....

SHIPPING DETAILS

Shipping method: ....
....

Tracking#: ....

Date shipped: ....

Subtotal: ....

Shipping cost: ....

Discount: ....

Total: ....

NOTES

....

....

....

ORDER FORM

Date:

Order#:

CUSTOMER DETAILS

Name: ....

Address: ....

Company: ....

Tel. .... E-mail: ....

ORDER DETAILS

No	Item(s) Description	QTY.	Price	Total
....	....	....	....	....
....	....	....	....	....
....	....	....	....	....
....	....	....	....	....
....	....	....	....	....
....	....	....	....	....
....	....	....	....	....

SHIPPING DETAILS

Shipping method: ....

....

Tracking#: ....

Date shipped: ....

Subtotal: ....

Shipping cost: ....

Discount: ....

Total: ....

NOTES

....

....

....

ORDER FORM

Date:

Order#:

CUSTOMER DETAILS

Name: ....

Address: ....

Company: ....

Tel. .... E-mail: ....

ORDER DETAILS

No	Item(s) Description	QTY.	Price	Total
....	....	....	....	....
....	....	....	....	....
....	....	....	....	....
....	....	....	....	....
....	....	....	....	....
....	....	....	....	....
....	....	....	....	....

SHIPPING DETAILS

Shipping method: ....

....

Tracking#: ....

Date shipped: ....

Subtotal: ....

Shipping cost: ....

Discount: ....

Total: ....

NOTES

....

....

....

ORDER FORM

Date: ....

Order#: ....

CUSTOMER DETAILS

Name: ....

Address: ....

Company: ....

Tel. .... E-mail: ....

ORDER DETAILS

No	Item(s) Description	QTY.	Price	Total
....	....	....	....	....
....	....	....	....	....
....	....	....	....	....
....	....	....	....	....
....	....	....	....	....
....	....	....	....	....
....	....	....	....	....

SHIPPING DETAILS

Shipping method: ....

....

Tracking#: ....

Date shipped: ....

Subtotal: ....

Shipping cost: ....

Discount: ....

Total: ....

NOTES

....

....

....

ORDER FORM

Date: ....

Order#: ....

CUSTOMER DETAILS

Name: ....

Address: ....

Company: ....

Tel. .... **E-mail:** ....

ORDER DETAILS

No	Item(s) Description	QTY.	Price	Total
....	....	....	....	....
....	....	....	....	....
....	....	....	....	....
....	....	....	....	....
....	....	....	....	....
....	....	....	....	....
....	....	....	....	....

SHIPPING DETAILS

Shipping method: ....

....

Tracking#: ....

Date shipped: ....

Subtotal: ....

Shipping cost: ....

Discount: ....

Total: ....

NOTES

....

....

....

ORDER FORM

Date:

Order#:

CUSTOMER DETAILS

Name: ....

Address: ....

Company: ....

Tel. .... E-mail: ....

ORDER DETAILS

No	Item(s) Description	QTY.	Price	Total
....	....	....	....	....
....	....	....	....	....
....	....	....	....	....
....	....	....	....	....
....	....	....	....	....
....	....	....	....	....
....	....	....	....	....

SHIPPING DETAILS

Shipping method: ....

....

Tracking#: ....

Date shipped: ....

Subtotal: ....

Shipping cost: ....

Discount: ....

Total: ....

NOTES

....

....

....

ORDER FORM

Date:

Order#:

CUSTOMER DETAILS

Name: ....

Address: ....

Company: ....

Tel. .... **E-mail:** ....

ORDER DETAILS

No	Item(s) Description	QTY.	Price	Total
....	....	....	....	....
....	....	....	....	....
....	....	....	....	....
....	....	....	....	....
....	....	....	....	....
....	....	....	....	....
....	....	....	....	....

SHIPPING DETAILS

Shipping method: ....

....

Tracking#: ....

Date shipped: ....

Subtotal: ....

Shipping cost: ....

Discount: ....

Total: ....

NOTES

....

....

....

ORDER FORM

Date:

Order#:

CUSTOMER DETAILS

Name: ....

Address: ....

Company: ....

Tel. .... E-mail: ....

ORDER DETAILS

No	Item(s) Description	QTY.	Price	Total
....	....	....	....	....
....	....	....	....	....
....	....	....	....	....
....	....	....	....	....
....	....	....	....	....
....	....	....	....	....
....	....	....	....	....

SHIPPING DETAILS

Shipping method: ....

....

Tracking#: ....

Date shipped: ....

Subtotal: ....

Shipping cost: ....

Discount: ....

Total: ....

NOTES

....

....

....

ORDER FORM

Date: ....

Order#: ....

CUSTOMER DETAILS

Name: ....

Address: ....

Company: ....

Tel. .... **E-mail:** ....

ORDER DETAILS

No	Item(s) Description	QTY.	Price	Total
....	....	....	....	....
....	....	....	....	....
....	....	....	....	....
....	....	....	....	....
....	....	....	....	....
....	....	....	....	....
....	....	....	....	....

SHIPPING DETAILS

Shipping method: ....

....

Tracking#: ....

Date shipped: ....

Subtotal: ....

Shipping cost: ....

Discount: ....

Total: ....

NOTES

....

....

....

ORDER FORM

Date:

Order#:

CUSTOMER DETAILS

Name: ....

Address: ....

Company: ....

Tel. .... E-mail: ....

ORDER DETAILS

No	Item(s) Description	QTY.	Price	Total
....	....	....	....	....
....	....	....	....	....
....	....	....	....	....
....	....	....	....	....
....	....	....	....	....
....	....	....	....	....
....	....	....	....	....

SHIPPING DETAILS

Shipping method: .... Subtotal: ....

.... Shipping cost: ....

Tracking#: .... Discount: ....

Date shipped: .... Total: ....

NOTES

....

....

....

ORDER FORM

Date: ....

Order#: ....

CUSTOMER DETAILS

Name: ....

Address: ....

Company: ....

Tel. .... **E-mail:** ....

ORDER DETAILS

No	Item(s) Description	QTY.	Price	Total
....	....	....	....	....
....	....	....	....	....
....	....	....	....	....
....	....	....	....	....
....	....	....	....	....
....	....	....	....	....
....	....	....	....	....

SHIPPING DETAILS

Shipping method: ....

....

Tracking#: ....

Date shipped: ....

Subtotal: ....

Shipping cost: ....

Discount: ....

Total: ....

NOTES

....

....

....

ORDER FORM

Date:

Order#:

CUSTOMER DETAILS

Name: ....

Address: ....

Company: ....

Tel. .... E-mail: ....

ORDER DETAILS

No	Item(s) Description	QTY.	Price	Total
....	....	....	....	....
....	....	....	....	....
....	....	....	....	....
....	....	....	....	....
....	....	....	....	....
....	....	....	....	....
....	....	....	....	....

SHIPPING DETAILS

Shipping method: ....

....

Tracking#: ....

Date shipped: ....

Subtotal: ....

Shipping cost: ....

Discount: ....

Total: ....

NOTES

....

....

....

ORDER FORM

Date: ....

Order#: ....

CUSTOMER DETAILS

Name: ....

Address: ....

Company: ....

Tel. .... **E-mail:** ....

ORDER DETAILS

No	Item(s) Description	QTY.	Price	Total
....	....	....	....	....
....	....	....	....	....
....	....	....	....	....
....	....	....	....	....
....	....	....	....	....
....	....	....	....	....
....	....	....	....	....

SHIPPING DETAILS

Shipping method: ....

....

Tracking#: ....

Date shipped: ....

Subtotal: ....

Shipping cost: ....

Discount: ....

Total: ....

NOTES

....

....

....

ORDER FORM

Date:

Order#:

CUSTOMER DETAILS

Name: ....

Address: ....

Company: ....

Tel. .... E-mail: ....

ORDER DETAILS

No	Item(s) Description	QTY.	Price	Total
....	....	....	....	....
....	....	....	....	....
....	....	....	....	....
....	....	....	....	....
....	....	....	....	....
....	....	....	....	....
....	....	....	....	....

SHIPPING DETAILS

Shipping method: ....

....

Tracking#: ....

Date shipped: ....

Subtotal: ....

Shipping cost: ....

Discount: ....

Total: ....

NOTES

....

....

ORDER FORM

Date: ....

Order#: ....

CUSTOMER DETAILS

Name: ....

Address: ....

Company: ....

Tel. .... **E-mail:** ....

ORDER DETAILS

No	Item(s) Description	QTY.	Price	Total
....	....	....	....	....
....	....	....	....	....
....	....	....	....	....
....	....	....	....	....
....	....	....	....	....
....	....	....	....	....
....	....	....	....	....

SHIPPING DETAILS

Shipping method: ....

....

Tracking#: ....

Date shipped: ....

Subtotal: ....

Shipping cost: ....

Discount: ....

Total: ....

NOTES

....

....

....

ORDER FORM

Date:

Order#:

CUSTOMER DETAILS

Name: ....

Address: ....

Company: ....

Tel. .... **E-mail:** ....

ORDER DETAILS

No	Item(s) Description	QTY.	Price	Total
....	....	....	....	....
....	....	....	....	....
....	....	....	....	....
....	....	....	....	....
....	....	....	....	....
....	....	....	....	....
....	....	....	....	....

SHIPPING DETAILS

Shipping method: ....

....

Tracking#: ....

Date shipped: ....

Subtotal: ....

Shipping cost: ....

Discount: ....

Total: ....

NOTES

....

....

....

ORDER FORM

Date: ....

Order#: ....

CUSTOMER DETAILS

Name: ....

Address: ....

Company: ....

Tel. .... **E-mail:** ....

ORDER DETAILS

No	Item(s) Description	QTY.	Price	Total
....	....	....	....	....
....	....	....	....	....
....	....	....	....	....
....	....	....	....	....
....	....	....	....	....
....	....	....	....	....
....	....	....	....	....

SHIPPING DETAILS

Shipping method: ....

....

Tracking#: ....

Date shipped: ....

Subtotal: ....

Shipping cost: ....

Discount: ....

Total: ....

NOTES

....

....

ORDER FORM

Date:

Order#:

CUSTOMER DETAILS

Name: ....

Address: ....

Company: ....

Tel. .... E-mail: ....

ORDER DETAILS

No	Item(s) Description	QTY.	Price	Total
....	....	....	....	....
....	....	....	....	....
....	....	....	....	....
....	....	....	....	....
....	....	....	....	....
....	....	....	....	....
....	....	....	....	....

SHIPPING DETAILS

Shipping method: ....

....

Tracking#: ....

Date shipped: ....

Subtotal: ....

Shipping cost: ....

Discount: ....

Total: ....

NOTES

....

....

....

ORDER FORM

Date: ....
Order#: ....

CUSTOMER DETAILS

Name: ....
Address: ....
Company: ....
Tel. .... **E-mail:** ....

ORDER DETAILS

No	Item(s) Description	QTY.	Price	Total
....	....	....	....	....
....	....	....	....	....
....	....	....	....	....
....	....	....	....	....
....	....	....	....	....
....	....	....	....	....
....	....	....	....	....

SHIPPING DETAILS

Shipping method: ....
....

Tracking#: ....

Date shipped: ....

Subtotal: ....

Shipping cost: ....

Discount: ....

Total: ....

NOTES

....
....
....

ORDER FORM

Date:

Order#:

CUSTOMER DETAILS

Name: ....

Address: ....

Company: ....

Tel. .... E-mail: ....

ORDER DETAILS

No	Item(s) Description	QTY.	Price	Total
....	....	....	....	....
....	....	....	....	....
....	....	....	....	....
....	....	....	....	....
....	....	....	....	....
....	....	....	....	....
....	....	....	....	....

SHIPPING DETAILS

Shipping method: ....

....

Subtotal: ....

Shipping cost: ....

Tracking#: ....

Discount: ....

Date shipped: ....

Total: ....

NOTES

....

....

....

ORDER FORM

Date: ....

Order#: ....

CUSTOMER DETAILS

Name: ....

Address: ....

Company: ....

Tel. .... **E-mail:** ....

ORDER DETAILS

No	Item(s) Description	QTY.	Price	Total
....	....	....	....	....
....	....	....	....	....
....	....	....	....	....
....	....	....	....	....
....	....	....	....	....
....	....	....	....	....
....	....	....	....	....

SHIPPING DETAILS

Shipping method: .... **Subtotal:** ....

.... **Shipping cost:** ....

Tracking#: .... **Discount:** ....

Date shipped: .... **Total:** ....

NOTES

....

....

ORDER FORM

Date: ....

Order#: ....

CUSTOMER DETAILS

Name: ....

Address: ....

Company: ....

Tel. .... E-mail: ....

ORDER DETAILS

No	Item(s) Description	QTY.	Price	Total
....	....	....	....	....
....	....	....	....	....
....	....	....	....	....
....	....	....	....	....
....	....	....	....	....
....	....	....	....	....
....	....	....	....	....

SHIPPING DETAILS

Shipping method: ....

....

Tracking#: ....

Date shipped: ....

Subtotal: ....

Shipping cost: ....

Discount: ....

Total: ....

NOTES

....

....

....

ORDER FORM

Date:

Order#:

CUSTOMER DETAILS

Name: ....

Address: ....

Company: ....

Tel. .... **E-mail:** ....

ORDER DETAILS

No	Item(s) Description	QTY.	Price	Total
....	....	....	....	....
....	....	....	....	....
....	....	....	....	....
....	....	....	....	....
....	....	....	....	....
....	....	....	....	....
....	....	....	....	....

SHIPPING DETAILS

Shipping method: .... **Subtotal:** ....

.... **Shipping cost:** ....

Tracking#: .... **Discount:** ....

Date shipped: .... **Total:** ....

NOTES

....

....

ORDER FORM

Date:

Order#:

CUSTOMER DETAILS

Name: ....

Address: ....

Company: ....

Tel. .... E-mail: ....

ORDER DETAILS

No	Item(s) Description	QTY.	Price	Total
....	....	....	....	....
....	....	....	....	....
....	....	....	....	....
....	....	....	....	....
....	....	....	....	....
....	....	....	....	....
....	....	....	....	....

SHIPPING DETAILS

Shipping method: ....

....

Tracking#: ....

Date shipped: ....

Subtotal: ....

Shipping cost: ....

Discount: ....

Total: ....

NOTES

....

....

....

ORDER FORM

Date: ....

Order#: ....

CUSTOMER DETAILS

Name: ....

Address: ....

Company: ....

Tel. .... **E-mail:** ....

ORDER DETAILS

No	Item(s) Description	QTY.	Price	Total
....	....	....	....	....
....	....	....	....	....
....	....	....	....	....
....	....	....	....	....
....	....	....	....	....
....	....	....	....	....
....	....	....	....	....

SHIPPING DETAILS

Shipping method: ....

....

Tracking#: ....

Date shipped: ....

Subtotal: ....

Shipping cost: ....

Discount: ....

Total: ....

NOTES

....

....

ORDER FORM

Date:

Order#:

CUSTOMER DETAILS

Name: ....

Address: ....

Company: ....

Tel. .... E-mail: ....

ORDER DETAILS

No	Item(s) Description	QTY.	Price	Total
....	....	....	....	....
....	....	....	....	....
....	....	....	....	....
....	....	....	....	....
....	....	....	....	....
....	....	....	....	....
....	....	....	....	....

SHIPPING DETAILS

Shipping method: ....

....

Tracking#: ....

Date shipped: ....

Subtotal: ....

Shipping cost: ....

Discount: ....

Total: ....

NOTES

....

....

....

ORDER FORM

Date:

Order#:

CUSTOMER DETAILS

Name: ....

Address: ....

Company: ....

Tel. .... **E-mail:** ....

ORDER DETAILS

No	Item(s) Description	QTY.	Price	Total
......	....	....	....	....
......	....	....	....	....
......	....	....	....	....
......	....	....	....	....
......	....	....	....	....
......	....	....	....	....
......	....	....	....	....

SHIPPING DETAILS

Shipping method: ....

....

Tracking#: ....

Date shipped: ....

Subtotal: ....

Shipping cost: ....

Discount: ....

Total: ....

NOTES

....

....

ORDER FORM

Date:

Order#:

CUSTOMER DETAILS

Name: ....

Address: ....

Company: ....

Tel. .... E-mail: ....

ORDER DETAILS

No	Item(s) Description	QTY.	Price	Total
....	....	....	....	....
....	....	....	....	....
....	....	....	....	....
....	....	....	....	....
....	....	....	....	....
....	....	....	....	....
....	....	....	....	....

SHIPPING DETAILS

Shipping method: ....

....

Tracking#: ....

Date shipped: ....

Subtotal: ....

Shipping cost: ....

Discount: ....

Total: ....

NOTES

....

....

....

ORDER FORM

Date: ....

Order#: ....

CUSTOMER DETAILS

Name: ....

Address: ....

Company: ....

Tel. .... **E-mail:** ....

ORDER DETAILS

No	Item(s) Description	QTY.	Price	Total
....	....	....	....	....
....	....	....	....	....
....	....	....	....	....
....	....	....	....	....
....	....	....	....	....
....	....	....	....	....
....	....	....	....	....

SHIPPING DETAILS

Shipping method: ....

....

Tracking#: ....

Date shipped: ....

Subtotal: ....

Shipping cost: ....

Discount: ....

Total: ....

NOTES

....

....

....

ORDER FORM

Date:

Order#:

CUSTOMER DETAILS

Name: ....

Address: ....

Company: ....

Tel. .... E-mail: ....

ORDER DETAILS

No	Item(s) Description	QTY.	Price	Total
....	....	....	....	....
....	....	....	....	....
....	....	....	....	....
....	....	....	....	....
....	....	....	....	....
....	....	....	....	....
....	....	....	....	....

SHIPPING DETAILS

Shipping method: ....

....

Tracking#: ....

Date shipped: ....

Subtotal: ....

Shipping cost: ....

Discount: ....

Total: ....

NOTES

....

....

....

ORDER FORM

Date:

Order#:

CUSTOMER DETAILS

Name: ....

Address: ....

Company: ....

Tel. .... **E-mail:** ....

ORDER DETAILS

No	Item(s) Description	QTY.	Price	Total
....	....	....	....	....
....	....	....	....	....
....	....	....	....	....
....	....	....	....	....
....	....	....	....	....
....	....	....	....	....
....	....	....	....	....

SHIPPING DETAILS

Shipping method: ....
....

Tracking#: ....

Date shipped: ....

Subtotal: ....

Shipping cost: ....

Discount: ....

Total: ....

NOTES

....

....

....

ORDER FORM

Date: ....

Order#: ....

CUSTOMER DETAILS

Name: ....

Address: ....

Company: ....

Tel. .... **E-mail:** ....

ORDER DETAILS

No	Item(s) Description	QTY.	Price	Total
....	....	....	....	....
....	....	....	....	....
....	....	....	....	....
....	....	....	....	....
....	....	....	....	....
....	....	....	....	....
....	....	....	....	....

SHIPPING DETAILS

Shipping method: ....

....

Tracking#: ....

Date shipped: ....

Subtotal: ....

Shipping cost: ....

Discount: ....

Total: ....

NOTES

....

....

....

ORDER FORM

Date: ....

Order#: ....

CUSTOMER DETAILS

Name: ....

Address: ....

Company: ....

Tel. .... **E-mail:** ....

ORDER DETAILS

No	Item(s) Description	QTY.	Price	Total
....	....	....	....	....
....	....	....	....	....
....	....	....	....	....
....	....	....	....	....
....	....	....	....	....
....	....	....	....	....
....	....	....	....	....

SHIPPING DETAILS

Shipping method: ....

....

Tracking#: ....

Date shipped: ....

Subtotal: ....

Shipping cost: ....

Discount: ....

Total: ....

NOTES

....

....

....

ORDER FORM

Date:

Order#:

CUSTOMER DETAILS

Name: ....

Address: ....

Company: ....

Tel. .... E-mail: ....

ORDER DETAILS

No	Item(s) Description	QTY.	Price	Total
....	....	....	....	....
....	....	....	....	....
....	....	....	....	....
....	....	....	....	....
....	....	....	....	....
....	....	....	....	....
....	....	....	....	....

SHIPPING DETAILS

Shipping method: ....

....

Tracking#: ....

Date shipped: ....

Subtotal: ....

Shipping cost: ....

Discount: ....

Total: ....

NOTES

....

....

....

ORDER FORM

Date: ....

Order#: ....

CUSTOMER DETAILS

Name: ....

Address: ....

Company: ....

Tel. .... **E-mail:** ....

ORDER DETAILS

No	Item(s) Description	QTY.	Price	Total
....	....	....	....	....
....	....	....	....	....
....	....	....	....	....
....	....	....	....	....
....	....	....	....	....
....	....	....	....	....
....	....	....	....	....

SHIPPING DETAILS

Shipping method: ....

....

Tracking#: ....

Date shipped: ....

Subtotal: ....

Shipping cost: ....

Discount: ....

Total: ....

NOTES

....

....

....

ORDER FORM

Date:

Order#:

CUSTOMER DETAILS

Name: ....

Address: ....

Company: ....

Tel. .... E-mail: ....

ORDER DETAILS

No	Item(s) Description	QTY.	Price	Total
....	....	....	....	....
....	....	....	....	....
....	....	....	....	....
....	....	....	....	....
....	....	....	....	....
....	....	....	....	....
....	....	....	....	....

SHIPPING DETAILS

Shipping method: ....   Subtotal: ....

....   Shipping cost: ....

Tracking#: ....   Discount: ....

Date shipped: ....   Total: ....

NOTES

....

....

....

ORDER FORM

Date:

Order#:

CUSTOMER DETAILS

Name: ....

Address: ....

Company: ....

Tel. .... **E-mail:** ....

ORDER DETAILS

No	Item(s) Description	QTY.	Price	Total
....	....	....	....	....
....	....	....	....	....
....	....	....	....	....
....	....	....	....	....
....	....	....	....	....
....	....	....	....	....
....	....	....	....	....

SHIPPING DETAILS

Shipping method: ....   **Subtotal:** ....

....   **Shipping cost:** ....

Tracking#: ....   **Discount:** ....

Date shipped: ....   **Total:** ....

NOTES

....

....

....

ORDER FORM

Date:

Order#:

CUSTOMER DETAILS

Name: ....

Address: ....

Company: ....

Tel. .... E-mail: ....

ORDER DETAILS

No	Item(s) Description	QTY.	Price	Total
....	....	....	....	....
....	....	....	....	....
....	....	....	....	....
....	....	....	....	....
....	....	....	....	....
....	....	....	....	....
....	....	....	....	....

SHIPPING DETAILS

Shipping method: ....   Subtotal: ....

....   Shipping cost: ....

Tracking#: ....   Discount: ....

Date shipped: ....   Total: ....

NOTES

....

....

....

ORDER FORM

Date:

Order#:

CUSTOMER DETAILS

Name: ....

Address: ....

Company: ....

Tel. .... E-mail: ....

ORDER DETAILS

No	Item(s) Description	QTY.	Price	Total
....	....	....	....	....
....	....	....	....	....
....	....	....	....	....
....	....	....	....	....
....	....	....	....	....
....	....	....	....	....
....	....	....	....	....

SHIPPING DETAILS

Shipping method: ....

....

Tracking#: ....

Date shipped: ....

Subtotal: ....

Shipping cost: ....

Discount: ....

Total: ....

NOTES

....

....

ORDER FORM

Date:

Order#:

CUSTOMER DETAILS

Name: ....

Address: ....

Company: ....

Tel. .... E-mail: ....

ORDER DETAILS

No	Item(s) Description	QTY.	Price	Total
....	....	....	....	....
....	....	....	....	....
....	....	....	....	....
....	....	....	....	....
....	....	....	....	....
....	....	....	....	....
....	....	....	....	....

SHIPPING DETAILS

Shipping method: ....

....

Tracking#: ....

Date shipped: ....

Subtotal: ....

Shipping cost: ....

Discount: ....

Total: ....

NOTES

....

....

....

ORDER FORM

Date:

Order#:

CUSTOMER DETAILS

Name: ....

Address: ....

Company: ....

Tel. .... **E-mail:** ....

ORDER DETAILS

No	Item(s) Description	QTY.	Price	Total
....	....	....	....	....
....	....	....	....	....
....	....	....	....	....
....	....	....	....	....
....	....	....	....	....
....	....	....	....	....
....	....	....	....	....

SHIPPING DETAILS

Shipping method: ....

....

Tracking#: ....

Date shipped: ....

Subtotal: ....

Shipping cost: ....

Discount: ....

Total: ....

NOTES

....

....

....

ORDER FORM

Date:

Order#:

CUSTOMER DETAILS

Name: ....

Address: ....

Company: ....

Tel. .... E-mail: ....

ORDER DETAILS

No	Item(s) Description	QTY.	Price	Total
....	....	....	....	....
....	....	....	....	....
....	....	....	....	....
....	....	....	....	....
....	....	....	....	....
....	....	....	....	....
....	....	....	....	....

SHIPPING DETAILS

Shipping method: ....

....

Tracking#: ....

Date shipped: ....

Subtotal: ....

Shipping cost: ....

Discount: ....

Total: ....

NOTES

....

....

....

ORDER FORM

Date:

Order#:

CUSTOMER DETAILS

Name: ....

Address: ....

Company: ....

Tel. .... **E-mail:** ....

ORDER DETAILS

No	Item(s) Description	QTY.	Price	Total
....	....	....	....	....
....	....	....	....	....
....	....	....	....	....
....	....	....	....	....
....	....	....	....	....
....	....	....	....	....
....	....	....	....	....

SHIPPING DETAILS

Shipping method: ....

....

Tracking#: ....

Date shipped: ....

Subtotal: ....

Shipping cost: ....

Discount: ....

Total: ....

NOTES

....

....

....

ORDER FORM

Date:

Order#:

CUSTOMER DETAILS

Name: ....

Address: ....

Company: ....

Tel. .... E-mail: ....

ORDER DETAILS

No	Item(s) Description	QTY.	Price	Total
....	....	....	....	....
....	....	....	....	....
....	....	....	....	....
....	....	....	....	....
....	....	....	....	....
....	....	....	....	....
....	....	....	....	....

SHIPPING DETAILS

Shipping method: ....   Subtotal: ....

....   Shipping cost: ....

Tracking#: ....   Discount: ....

Date shipped: ....   Total: ....

NOTES

....

....

....

ORDER FORM

Date:

Order#:

CUSTOMER DETAILS

Name: ....

Address: ....

Company: ....

Tel. .... **E-mail:** ....

ORDER DETAILS

No	Item(s) Description	QTY.	Price	Total
....	....	....	....	....
....	....	....	....	....
....	....	....	....	....
....	....	....	....	....
....	....	....	....	....
....	....	....	....	....
....	....	....	....	....

SHIPPING DETAILS

Shipping method: ....

....

Tracking#: ....

Date shipped: ....

Subtotal: ....

Shipping cost: ....

Discount: ....

Total: ....

NOTES

....

....

ORDER FORM

Date:

Order#:

CUSTOMER DETAILS

Name: ....

Address: ....

Company: ....

Tel. .... E-mail: ....

ORDER DETAILS

No	Item(s) Description	QTY.	Price	Total
....	....	....	....	....
....	....	....	....	....
....	....	....	....	....
....	....	....	....	....
....	....	....	....	....
....	....	....	....	....
....	....	....	....	....

SHIPPING DETAILS

Shipping method: ....

....

Tracking#: ....

Date shipped: ....

Subtotal: ....

Shipping cost: ....

Discount: ....

Total: ....

NOTES

....

....

....

ORDER FORM

Date: ....

Order#: ....

CUSTOMER DETAILS

Name: ....

Address: ....

Company: ....

Tel. .... **E-mail:** ....

ORDER DETAILS

No	Item(s) Description	QTY.	Price	Total
......	....	....	....	....
......	....	....	....	....
......	....	....	....	....
......	....	....	....	....
......	....	....	....	....
......	....	....	....	....
......	....	....	....	....

SHIPPING DETAILS

Shipping method: ....

....

Tracking#: ....

Date shipped: ....

Subtotal: ....

Shipping cost: ....

Discount: ....

Total: ....

NOTES

....

....

....

ORDER FORM

Date:

Order#:

CUSTOMER DETAILS

Name: ....

Address: ....

Company: ....

Tel. .... E-mail: ....

ORDER DETAILS

No	Item(s) Description	QTY.	Price	Total
....	....	....	....	....
....	....	....	....	....
....	....	....	....	....
....	....	....	....	....
....	....	....	....	....
....	....	....	....	....
....	....	....	....	....

SHIPPING DETAILS

Shipping method: ....

....

Tracking#: ....

Date shipped: ....

Subtotal: ....

Shipping cost: ....

Discount: ....

Total: ....

NOTES

....

....

....

ORDER FORM

Date:

Order#:

CUSTOMER DETAILS

Name: ....

Address: ....

Company: ....

Tel. .... **E-mail:** ....

ORDER DETAILS

No	Item(s) Description	QTY.	Price	Total
....	....	....	....	....
....	....	....	....	....
....	....	....	....	....
....	....	....	....	....
....	....	....	....	....
....	....	....	....	....
....	....	....	....	....

SHIPPING DETAILS

Shipping method: ....

....

Tracking#: ....

Date shipped: ....

Subtotal: ....

Shipping cost: ....

Discount: ....

Total: ....

NOTES

....

....

....

ORDER FORM

Date:

Order#:

CUSTOMER DETAILS

Name: ....

Address: ....

Company: ....

Tel. .... E-mail: ....

ORDER DETAILS

No	Item(s) Description	QTY.	Price	Total
....	....	....	....	....
....	....	....	....	....
....	....	....	....	....
....	....	....	....	....
....	....	....	....	....
....	....	....	....	....
....	....	....	....	....

SHIPPING DETAILS

Shipping method: ....   Subtotal: ....

....   Shipping cost: ....

Tracking#: ....   Discount: ....

Date shipped: ....   Total: ....

NOTES

....

....

....

ORDER FORM

Date: ....

Order#: ....

CUSTOMER DETAILS

Name: ....

Address: ....

Company: ....

Tel. .... **E-mail:** ....

ORDER DETAILS

No	Item(s) Description	QTY.	Price	Total
....	....	....	....	....
....	....	....	....	....
....	....	....	....	....
....	....	....	....	....
....	....	....	....	....
....	....	....	....	....
....	....	....	....	....

SHIPPING DETAILS

Shipping method: ....

....

Tracking#: ....

Date shipped: ....

Subtotal: ....

Shipping cost: ....

Discount: ....

Total: ....

NOTES

....

....

ORDER FORM

Date:

Order#:

CUSTOMER DETAILS

Name: ....

Address: ....

Company: ....

Tel. .... E-mail: ....

ORDER DETAILS

No	Item(s) Description	QTY.	Price	Total
....	....	....	....	....
....	....	....	....	....
....	....	....	....	....
....	....	....	....	....
....	....	....	....	....
....	....	....	....	....
....	....	....	....	....

SHIPPING DETAILS

Shipping method: .... Subtotal: ....

.... Shipping cost: ....

Tracking#: .... Discount: ....

Date shipped: .... Total: ....

NOTES

....

....

....

ORDER FORM

Date: ....

Order#: ....

CUSTOMER DETAILS

Name: ....

Address: ....

Company: ....

Tel. .... E-mail: ....

ORDER DETAILS

No	Item(s) Description	QTY.	Price	Total
....	....	....	....	....
....	....	....	....	....
....	....	....	....	....
....	....	....	....	....
....	....	....	....	....
....	....	....	....	....
....	....	....	....	....

SHIPPING DETAILS

Shipping method: ....

....

Tracking#: ....

Date shipped: ....

Subtotal: ....

Shipping cost: ....

Discount: ....

Total: ....

NOTES

....

....

....

ORDER FORM

Date:

Order#:

CUSTOMER DETAILS

Name: ....

Address: ....

Company: ....

Tel. .... E-mail: ....

ORDER DETAILS

No	Item(s) Description	QTY.	Price	Total
....	....	....	....	....
....	....	....	....	....
....	....	....	....	....
....	....	....	....	....
....	....	....	....	....
....	....	....	....	....
....	....	....	....	....

SHIPPING DETAILS

Shipping method: ....   Subtotal: ....

....   Shipping cost: ....

Tracking#: ....   Discount: ....

Date shipped: ....   Total: ....

NOTES

....

....

....

ORDER FORM

Date: ....
Order#: ....

CUSTOMER DETAILS

Name: ....

Address: ....

Company: ....

Tel. .... E-mail: ....

ORDER DETAILS

No	Item(s) Description	QTY.	Price	Total
....	....	....	....	....
....	....	....	....	....
....	....	....	....	....
....	....	....	....	....
....	....	....	....	....
....	....	....	....	....
....	....	....	....	....

SHIPPING DETAILS

Shipping method: ....

....

Tracking#: ....

Date shipped: ....

Subtotal: ....

Shipping cost: ....

Discount: ....

Total: ....

NOTES

....

....

....

ORDER FORM

Date:

Order#:

CUSTOMER DETAILS

Name: ....

Address: ....

Company: ....

Tel. .... E-mail: ....

ORDER DETAILS

No	Item(s) Description	QTY.	Price	Total
....	....	....	....	....
....	....	....	....	....
....	....	....	....	....
....	....	....	....	....
....	....	....	....	....
....	....	....	....	....
....	....	....	....	....

SHIPPING DETAILS

Shipping method: ....

....

Tracking#: ....

Date shipped: ....

Subtotal: ....

Shipping cost: ....

Discount: ....

Total: ....

NOTES

....

....

....

ORDER FORM

Date: ....

Order#: ....

CUSTOMER DETAILS

Name: ....

Address: ....

Company: ....

Tel. .... **E-mail:** ....

ORDER DETAILS

No	Item(s) Description	QTY.	Price	Total
....	....	....	....	....
....	....	....	....	....
....	....	....	....	....
....	....	....	....	....
....	....	....	....	....
....	....	....	....	....
....	....	....	....	....

SHIPPING DETAILS

Shipping method: ....

....

Tracking#: ....

Date shipped: ....

Subtotal: ....

Shipping cost: ....

Discount: ....

Total: ....

NOTES

....

....

....

ORDER FORM

Date:

Order#:

CUSTOMER DETAILS

Name: ....

Address: ....

Company: ....

Tel. .... E-mail: ....

ORDER DETAILS

No	Item(s) Description	QTY.	Price	Total
....	....	....	....	....
....	....	....	....	....
....	....	....	....	....
....	....	....	....	....
....	....	....	....	....
....	....	....	....	....
....	....	....	....	....

SHIPPING DETAILS

Shipping method: ....

....

Tracking#: ....

Date shipped: ....

Subtotal: ....

Shipping cost: ....

Discount: ....

Total: ....

NOTES

....

....

....

ORDER FORM

Date:

Order#:

CUSTOMER DETAILS

Name: ....

Address: ....

Company: ....

Tel. .... **E-mail:** ....

ORDER DETAILS

No	Item(s) Description	QTY.	Price	Total
....	....	....	....	....
....	....	....	....	....
....	....	....	....	....
....	....	....	....	....
....	....	....	....	....
....	....	....	....	....
....	....	....	....	....

SHIPPING DETAILS

Shipping method: ....

....

Tracking#: ....

Date shipped: ....

Subtotal: ....

Shipping cost: ....

Discount: ....

Total: ....

NOTES

....

....

....

ORDER FORM

Date:

Order#:

CUSTOMER DETAILS

Name: ....

Address: ....

Company: ....

Tel. .... E-mail: ....

ORDER DETAILS

No	Item(s) Description	QTY.	Price	Total
....	....	....	....	....
....	....	....	....	....
....	....	....	....	....
....	....	....	....	....
....	....	....	....	....
....	....	....	....	....
....	....	....	....	....

SHIPPING DETAILS

Shipping method: ....

Subtotal: ....

....

Shipping cost: ....

Tracking#: ....

Discount: ....

Date shipped: ....

Total: ....

NOTES

....

....

....

ORDER FORM

Date: ....

Order#: ....

CUSTOMER DETAILS

Name: ....

Address: ....

Company: ....

Tel. .... **E-mail:** ....

ORDER DETAILS

No	Item(s) Description	QTY.	Price	Total
....	....	....	....	....
....	....	....	....	....
....	....	....	....	....
....	....	....	....	....
....	....	....	....	....
....	....	....	....	....
....	....	....	....	....

SHIPPING DETAILS

Shipping method: ....

....

Tracking#: ....

Date shipped: ....

Subtotal: ....

Shipping cost: ....

Discount: ....

Total: ....

NOTES

....

....

....

ORDER FORM

Date:

Order#:

CUSTOMER DETAILS

Name: ....

Address: ....

Company: ....

Tel. .... **E-mail:** ....

ORDER DETAILS

No	Item(s) Description	QTY.	Price	Total
....	....	....	....	....
....	....	....	....	....
....	....	....	....	....
....	....	....	....	....
....	....	....	....	....
....	....	....	....	....
....	....	....	....	....

SHIPPING DETAILS

Shipping method: ....

Subtotal: ....

....

Shipping cost: ....

Tracking#: ....

Discount: ....

Date shipped: ....

Total: ....

NOTES

....

....

....

ORDER FORM

Date:

Order#:

CUSTOMER DETAILS

Name: ....

Address: ....

Company: ....

Tel. .... **E-mail:** ....

ORDER DETAILS

No	Item(s) Description	QTY.	Price	Total
....	....	....	....	....
....	....	....	....	....
....	....	....	....	....
....	....	....	....	....
....	....	....	....	....
....	....	....	....	....
....	....	....	....	....

SHIPPING DETAILS

Shipping method: .... **Subtotal:** ....

.... **Shipping cost:** ....

Tracking#: .... **Discount:** ....

Date shipped: .... **Total:** ....

NOTES

....

....

ORDER FORM

Date:

Order#:

CUSTOMER DETAILS

Name: ....

Address: ....

Company: ....

Tel. .... **E-mail:** ....

ORDER DETAILS

No	Item(s) Description	QTY.	Price	Total
....	....	....	....	....
....	....	....	....	....
....	....	....	....	....
....	....	....	....	....
....	....	....	....	....
....	....	....	....	....
....	....	....	....	....

SHIPPING DETAILS

Shipping method: ....

....

Tracking#: ....

Date shipped: ....

Subtotal: ....

Shipping cost: ....

Discount: ....

Total: ....

NOTES

....

....

....

ORDER FORM

Date:

Order#:

CUSTOMER DETAILS

Name: ....

Address: ....

Company: ....

Tel. .... **E-mail:** ....

ORDER DETAILS

No	Item(s) Description	QTY.	Price	Total
....	....	....	....	....
....	....	....	....	....
....	....	....	....	....
....	....	....	....	....
....	....	....	....	....
....	....	....	....	....
....	....	....	....	....

SHIPPING DETAILS

Shipping method: ....

....

Tracking#: ....

Date shipped: ....

Subtotal: ....

Shipping cost: ....

Discount: ....

Total: ....

NOTES

....

....

ORDER FORM

Date:

Order#:

CUSTOMER DETAILS

Name: ....

Address: ....

Company: ....

Tel. .... **E-mail:** ....

ORDER DETAILS

No	Item(s) Description	QTY.	Price	Total
....	....	....	....	....
....	....	....	....	....
....	....	....	....	....
....	....	....	....	....
....	....	....	....	....
....	....	....	....	....
....	....	....	....	....

SHIPPING DETAILS

Shipping method: ....

....

Tracking#: ....

Date shipped: ....

Subtotal: ....

Shipping cost: ....

Discount: ....

Total: ....

NOTES

....

....

....

ORDER FORM

Date: ....

Order#: ....

CUSTOMER DETAILS

Name: ....

Address: ....

Company: ....

Tel. .... E-mail: ....

ORDER DETAILS

No	Item(s) Description	QTY.	Price	Total
....	....	....	....	....
....	....	....	....	....
....	....	....	....	....
....	....	....	....	....
....	....	....	....	....
....	....	....	....	....
....	....	....	....	....

SHIPPING DETAILS

Shipping method: ....

....

Tracking#: ....

Date shipped: ....

Subtotal: ....

Shipping cost: ....

Discount: ....

Total: ....

NOTES

....

....

ORDER FORM

Date:

Order#:

CUSTOMER DETAILS

Name: ....

Address: ....

Company: ....

Tel. .... **E-mail:** ....

ORDER DETAILS

No	Item(s) Description	QTY.	Price	Total
....	....	....	....	....
....	....	....	....	....
....	....	....	....	....
....	....	....	....	....
....	....	....	....	....
....	....	....	....	....
....	....	....	....	....

SHIPPING DETAILS

Shipping method: ....

....

Tracking#: ....

Date shipped: ....

Subtotal: ....

Shipping cost: ....

Discount: ....

Total: ....

NOTES

....

....

ORDER FORM

Date: ....

Order#: ....

CUSTOMER DETAILS

Name: ....

Address: ....

Company: ....

Tel. .... **E-mail:** ....

ORDER DETAILS

No	Item(s) Description	QTY.	Price	Total
....	....	....	....	....
....	....	....	....	....
....	....	....	....	....
....	....	....	....	....
....	....	....	....	....
....	....	....	....	....
....	....	....	....	....

SHIPPING DETAILS

Shipping method: ....

....

Tracking#: ....

Date shipped: ....

Subtotal: ....

Shipping cost: ....

Discount: ....

Total: ....

NOTES

....

....

....

ORDER FORM

Date:

Order#:

CUSTOMER DETAILS

Name: ....

Address: ....

Company: ....

Tel. .... **E-mail:** ....

ORDER DETAILS

No	Item(s) Description	QTY.	Price	Total
....	....	....	....	....
....	....	....	....	....
....	....	....	....	....
....	....	....	....	....
....	....	....	....	....
....	....	....	....	....
....	....	....	....	....

SHIPPING DETAILS

Shipping method: ....

Subtotal: ....

....

Shipping cost: ....

Tracking#: ....

Discount: ....

Date shipped: ....

Total: ....

NOTES

....

....

ORDER FORM

Date:

Order#:

CUSTOMER DETAILS

Name:

Address:

Company:

Tel. .... E-mail:

ORDER DETAILS

No	Item(s) Description	QTY.	Price	Total
....	....	....	....	....
....	....	....	....	....
....	....	....	....	....
....	....	....	....	....
....	....	....	....	....
....	....	....	....	....
....	....	....	....	....

SHIPPING DETAILS

Shipping method: ....

....

Tracking#: ....

Date shipped: ....

Subtotal: ....

Shipping cost: ....

Discount: ....

Total: ....

NOTES

....

....

ORDER FORM

Date:

Order#:

CUSTOMER DETAILS

Name: ....

Address: ....

Company: ....

Tel. .... E-mail: ....

ORDER DETAILS

No	Item(s) Description	QTY.	Price	Total
....	....	....	....	....
....	....	....	....	....
....	....	....	....	....
....	....	....	....	....
....	....	....	....	....
....	....	....	....	....
....	....	....	....	....

SHIPPING DETAILS

Shipping method: ....

....

Tracking#: ....

Date shipped: ....

Subtotal: ....

Shipping cost: ....

Discount: ....

Total: ....

NOTES

....

....

....

ORDER FORM

Date: ....

Order#: ....

CUSTOMER DETAILS

Name: ....

Address: ....

Company: ....

Tel. .... **E-mail:** ....

ORDER DETAILS

No	Item(s) Description	QTY.	Price	Total
....	....	....	....	....
....	....	....	....	....
....	....	....	....	....
....	....	....	....	....
....	....	....	....	....
....	....	....	....	....
....	....	....	....	....

SHIPPING DETAILS

Shipping method: ....

....

Tracking#: ....

Date shipped: ....

Subtotal: ....

Shipping cost: ....

Discount: ....

Total: ....

NOTES

....

....

ORDER FORM

Date:

Order#:

CUSTOMER DETAILS

Name: ....

Address: ....

Company: ....

Tel. .... **E-mail:** ....

ORDER DETAILS

No	Item(s) Description	QTY.	Price	Total
....	....	....	....	....
....	....	....	....	....
....	....	....	....	....
....	....	....	....	....
....	....	....	....	....
....	....	....	....	....
....	....	....	....	....

SHIPPING DETAILS

Shipping method: .... **Subtotal:** ....

.... **Shipping cost:** ....

Tracking#: .... **Discount:** ....

Date shipped: .... **Total:** ....

NOTES

....

....

....

ORDER FORM

Date: ....

Order#: ....

CUSTOMER DETAILS

Name: ....

Address: ....

Company: ....

Tel. .... **E-mail:** ....

ORDER DETAILS

No	Item(s) Description	QTY.	Price	Total
....	....	....	....	....
....	....	....	....	....
....	....	....	....	....
....	....	....	....	....
....	....	....	....	....
....	....	....	....	....
....	....	....	....	....

SHIPPING DETAILS

Shipping method: ....

....

Tracking#: ....

Date shipped: ....

Subtotal: ....

Shipping cost: ....

Discount: ....

Total: ....

NOTES

....

....

ORDER FORM

Date:

Order#:

CUSTOMER DETAILS

Name: ....

Address: ....

Company: ....

Tel. .... **E-mail:** ....

ORDER DETAILS

No	Item(s) Description	QTY.	Price	Total
....	....	....	....	....
....	....	....	....	....
....	....	....	....	....
....	....	....	....	....
....	....	....	....	....
....	....	....	....	....
....	....	....	....	....

SHIPPING DETAILS

Shipping method: ....

....

Tracking#: ....

Date shipped: ....

Subtotal: ....

Shipping cost: ....

Discount: ....

Total: ....

NOTES

....

....

ORDER FORM

Date: ....

Order#: ....

CUSTOMER DETAILS

Name: ....

Address: ....

Company: ....

Tel. .... **E-mail:** ....

ORDER DETAILS

No	Item(s) Description	QTY.	Price	Total
....	....	....	....	....
....	....	....	....	....
....	....	....	....	....
....	....	....	....	....
....	....	....	....	....
....	....	....	....	....
....	....	....	....	....

SHIPPING DETAILS

Shipping method: ....

....

Tracking#: ....

Date shipped: ....

Subtotal: ....

Shipping cost: ....

Discount: ....

Total: ....

NOTES

....

....

....

ORDER FORM

Date:

Order#:

CUSTOMER DETAILS

Name: ....

Address: ....

Company: ....

Tel. .... **E-mail:** ....

ORDER DETAILS

No	Item(s) Description	QTY.	Price	Total
....	....	....	....	....
....	....	....	....	....
....	....	....	....	....
....	....	....	....	....
....	....	....	....	....
....	....	....	....	....
....	....	....	....	....

SHIPPING DETAILS

Shipping method: ....

....

Tracking#: ....

Date shipped: ....

Subtotal: ....

Shipping cost: ....

Discount: ....

Total: ....

NOTES

....

....

ORDER FORM

Date: ....

Order#: ....

CUSTOMER DETAILS

Name: ....

Address: ....

Company: ....

Tel. .... **E-mail:** ....

ORDER DETAILS

No	Item(s) Description	QTY.	Price	Total
....	....	....	....	....
....	....	....	....	....
....	....	....	....	....
....	....	....	....	....
....	....	....	....	....
....	....	....	....	....
....	....	....	....	....

SHIPPING DETAILS

Shipping method: ....

....

Tracking#: ....

Date shipped: ....

Subtotal: ....

Shipping cost: ....

Discount: ....

Total: ....

NOTES

....

....

....

ORDER FORM

Date:

Order#:

CUSTOMER DETAILS

Name: ....

Address: ....

Company: ....

Tel. .... **E-mail:** ....

ORDER DETAILS

No	Item(s) Description	QTY.	Price	Total
....	....	....	....	....
....	....	....	....	....
....	....	....	....	....
....	....	....	....	....
....	....	....	....	....
....	....	....	....	....
....	....	....	....	....

SHIPPING DETAILS

Shipping method: ....

....

Tracking#: ....

Date shipped: ....

Subtotal: ....

Shipping cost: ....

Discount: ....

Total: ....

NOTES

....

....

....

ORDER FORM

Date:

Order#:

CUSTOMER DETAILS

Name: ....

Address: ....

Company: ....

Tel. .... **E-mail:** ....

ORDER DETAILS

No	Item(s) Description	QTY.	Price	Total
....	....	....	....	....
....	....	....	....	....
....	....	....	....	....
....	....	....	....	....
....	....	....	....	....
....	....	....	....	....
....	....	....	....	....

SHIPPING DETAILS

Shipping method: ....   **Subtotal:** ....

....   **Shipping cost:** ....

Tracking#: ....   **Discount:** ....

Date shipped: ....   **Total:** ....

NOTES

....

....

ORDER FORM

Date:

Order#:

CUSTOMER DETAILS

Name: ....

Address: ....

Company: ....

Tel. .... E-mail: ....

ORDER DETAILS

No	Item(s) Description	QTY.	Price	Total
....	....	....	....	....
....	....	....	....	....
....	....	....	....	....
....	....	....	....	....
....	....	....	....	....
....	....	....	....	....
....	....	....	....	....

SHIPPING DETAILS

Shipping method: ....

....

Tracking#: ....

Date shipped: ....

Subtotal: ....

Shipping cost: ....

Discount: ....

Total: ....

NOTES

....

....

....

ORDER FORM

Date:

Order#:

CUSTOMER DETAILS

Name: ....

Address: ....

Company: ....

Tel. .... **E-mail:** ....

ORDER DETAILS

No	Item(s) Description	QTY.	Price	Total
....	....	....	....	....
....	....	....	....	....
....	....	....	....	....
....	....	....	....	....
....	....	....	....	....
....	....	....	....	....
....	....	....	....	....

SHIPPING DETAILS

Shipping method: ....

....

Tracking#: ....

Date shipped: ....

Subtotal: ....

Shipping cost: ....

Discount: ....

Total: ....

NOTES

....

....

....

ORDER FORM

Date:

Order#:

CUSTOMER DETAILS

Name: ....

Address: ....

Company: ....

Tel. .... **E-mail:** ....

ORDER DETAILS

No	Item(s) Description	QTY.	Price	Total
....	....	....	....	....
....	....	....	....	....
....	....	....	....	....
....	....	....	....	....
....	....	....	....	....
....	....	....	....	....
....	....	....	....	....

SHIPPING DETAILS

Shipping method: ....

....

Tracking#: ....

Date shipped: ....

Subtotal: ....

Shipping cost: ....

Discount: ....

Total: ....

NOTES

....

....

....

ORDER FORM

Date: ....

Order#: ....

CUSTOMER DETAILS

Name: ....

Address: ....

Company: ....

Tel. .... **E-mail:** ....

ORDER DETAILS

No	Item(s) Description	QTY.	Price	Total
....	....	....	....	....
....	....	....	....	....
....	....	....	....	....
....	....	....	....	....
....	....	....	....	....
....	....	....	....	....
....	....	....	....	....

SHIPPING DETAILS

Shipping method: ....

....

Tracking#: ....

Date shipped: ....

Subtotal: ....

Shipping cost: ....

Discount: ....

Total: ....

NOTES

....

....

ORDER FORM

Date:

Order#:

CUSTOMER DETAILS

Name: ....

Address: ....

Company: ....

Tel. .... **E-mail:** ....

ORDER DETAILS

No	Item(s) Description	QTY.	Price	Total
......	....	....	....	....
......	....	....	....	....
......	....	....	....	....
......	....	....	....	....
......	....	....	....	....
......	....	....	....	....
......	....	....	....	....

SHIPPING DETAILS

Shipping method: ....

....

Tracking#: ....

Date shipped: ....

Subtotal: ....

Shipping cost: ....

Discount: ....

Total: ....

NOTES

....

....

ORDER FORM

Date:

Order#:

CUSTOMER DETAILS

Name: ....

Address: ....

Company: ....

Tel. .... **E-mail:** ....

ORDER DETAILS

No	Item(s) Description	QTY.	Price	Total
....	....	....	....	....
....	....	....	....	....
....	....	....	....	....
....	....	....	....	....
....	....	....	....	....
....	....	....	....	....
....	....	....	....	....

SHIPPING DETAILS

Shipping method: ....

....

Tracking#: ....

Date shipped: ....

Subtotal: ....

Shipping cost: ....

Discount: ....

Total: ....

NOTES

....

....

ORDER FORM

Date:

Order#:

CUSTOMER DETAILS

Name: ....

Address: ....

Company: ....

Tel. .... **E-mail:** ....

ORDER DETAILS

No	Item(s) Description	QTY.	Price	Total
....	....	....	....	....
....	....	....	....	....
....	....	....	....	....
....	....	....	....	....
....	....	....	....	....
....	....	....	....	....
....	....	....	....	....

SHIPPING DETAILS

Shipping method: ....

....

Tracking#: ....

Date shipped: ....

Subtotal: ....

Shipping cost: ....

Discount: ....

Total: ....

NOTES

....

....

ORDER FORM

Date:

Order#:

CUSTOMER DETAILS

Name: ....

Address: ....

Company: ....

Tel. .... **E-mail:** ....

ORDER DETAILS

No	Item(s) Description	QTY.	Price	Total
....	....	....	....	....
....	....	....	....	....
....	....	....	....	....
....	....	....	....	....
....	....	....	....	....
....	....	....	....	....
....	....	....	....	....

SHIPPING DETAILS

Shipping method: ....   **Subtotal:** ....

....   **Shipping cost:** ....

Tracking#: ....   **Discount:** ....

Date shipped: ....   **Total:** ....

NOTES

....

....

ORDER FORM

Date:

Order#:

CUSTOMER DETAILS

Name: ....

Address: ....

Company: ....

Tel. .... **E-mail:** ....

ORDER DETAILS

No	Item(s) Description	QTY.	Price	Total
....	....	....	....	....
....	....	....	....	....
....	....	....	....	....
....	....	....	....	....
....	....	....	....	....
....	....	....	....	....
....	....	....	....	....

SHIPPING DETAILS

Shipping method: ....

....

Tracking#: ....

Date shipped: ....

Subtotal: ....

Shipping cost: ....

Discount: ....

Total: ....

NOTES

....

....

....

ORDER FORM

Date:

Order#:

CUSTOMER DETAILS

Name: ....

Address: ....

Company: ....

Tel. .... **E-mail:** ....

ORDER DETAILS

No	Item(s) Description	QTY.	Price	Total
....	....	....	....	....
....	....	....	....	....
....	....	....	....	....
....	....	....	....	....
....	....	....	....	....
....	....	....	....	....
....	....	....	....	....

SHIPPING DETAILS

Shipping method: ....

....

Tracking#: ....

Date shipped: ....

Subtotal: ....

Shipping cost: ....

Discount: ....

Total: ....

NOTES

....

....

ORDER FORM

Date:

Order#:

CUSTOMER DETAILS

Name: ....

Address: ....

Company: ....

Tel. .... E-mail: ....

ORDER DETAILS

No	Item(s) Description	QTY.	Price	Total
....	....	....	....	....
....	....	....	....	....
....	....	....	....	....
....	....	....	....	....
....	....	....	....	....
....	....	....	....	....
....	....	....	....	....

SHIPPING DETAILS

Shipping method: ....

....

Tracking#: ....

Date shipped: ....

Subtotal: ....

Shipping cost: ....

Discount: ....

Total: ....

NOTES

....

....

....

ORDER FORM

Date:

Order#:

CUSTOMER DETAILS

Name: ....

Address: ....

Company: ....

Tel. .... **E-mail:** ....

ORDER DETAILS

No	Item(s) Description	QTY.	Price	Total
....	....	....	....	....
....	....	....	....	....
....	....	....	....	....
....	....	....	....	....
....	....	....	....	....
....	....	....	....	....
....	....	....	....	....

SHIPPING DETAILS

Shipping method: ....

....

Tracking#: ....

Date shipped: ....

Subtotal: ....

Shipping cost: ....

Discount: ....

Total: ....

NOTES

....

....

ORDER FORM

Date:

Order#:

CUSTOMER DETAILS

Name: ....

Address: ....

Company: ....

Tel. .... **E-mail:** ....

ORDER DETAILS

No	Item(s) Description	QTY.	Price	Total
....	....	....	....	....
....	....	....	....	....
....	....	....	....	....
....	....	....	....	....
....	....	....	....	....
....	....	....	....	....
....	....	....	....	....

SHIPPING DETAILS

Shipping method: ....

Subtotal: ....

....

Shipping cost: ....

Tracking#: ....

Discount: ....

Date shipped: ....

Total: ....

NOTES

....

....

ORDER FORM

Date:

Order#:

CUSTOMER DETAILS

Name: ....

Address: ....

Company: ....

Tel. .... **E-mail:** ....

ORDER DETAILS

No	Item(s) Description	QTY.	Price	Total
....	....	....	....	....
....	....	....	....	....
....	....	....	....	....
....	....	....	....	....
....	....	....	....	....
....	....	....	....	....
....	....	....	....	....

SHIPPING DETAILS

Shipping method: ....

....

Tracking#: ....

Date shipped: ....

Subtotal: ....

Shipping cost: ....

Discount: ....

Total: ....

NOTES

....

....

ORDER FORM

Date:

Order#:

CUSTOMER DETAILS

Name: ....

Address: ....

Company: ....

Tel. .... E-mail: ....

ORDER DETAILS

No	Item(s) Description	QTY.	Price	Total
......	....	....	....	....
......	....	....	....	....
......	....	....	....	....
......	....	....	....	....
......	....	....	....	....
......	....	....	....	....
......	....	....	....	....

SHIPPING DETAILS

Shipping method: ....

....

Tracking#: ....

Date shipped: ....

Subtotal: ....

Shipping cost: ....

Discount: ....

Total: ....

NOTES

....

....

....

ORDER FORM

Date:

Order#:

CUSTOMER DETAILS

Name: ....

Address: ....

Company: ....

Tel. .... **E-mail:** ....

ORDER DETAILS

No	Item(s) Description	QTY.	Price	Total
....	....	....	....	....
....	....	....	....	....
....	....	....	....	....
....	....	....	....	....
....	....	....	....	....
....	....	....	....	....
....	....	....	....	....

SHIPPING DETAILS

Shipping method: .... **Subtotal:** ....

.... **Shipping cost:** ....

Tracking#: .... **Discount:** ....

Date shipped: .... **Total:** ....

NOTES

....

....

ORDER FORM

Date:

Order#:

CUSTOMER DETAILS

Name: ....

Address: ....

Company: ....

Tel. .... E-mail: ....

ORDER DETAILS

No	Item(s) Description	QTY.	Price	Total
......	....	....	....	....
......	....	....	....	....
......	....	....	....	....
......	....	....	....	....
......	....	....	....	....
......	....	....	....	....
......	....	....	....	....

SHIPPING DETAILS

Shipping method: .... Subtotal: ....

.... Shipping cost: ....

Tracking#: .... Discount: ....

Date shipped: .... Total: ....

NOTES

....

....

....

ORDER FORM

Date:

Order#:

CUSTOMER DETAILS

Name: ....

Address: ....

Company: ....

Tel. .... E-mail: ....

ORDER DETAILS

No	Item(s) Description	QTY.	Price	Total
....	....	....	....	....
....	....	....	....	....
....	....	....	....	....
....	....	....	....	....
....	....	....	....	....
....	....	....	....	....
....	....	....	....	....

SHIPPING DETAILS

Shipping method: ....

....

Tracking#: ....

Date shipped: ....

Subtotal: ....

Shipping cost: ....

Discount: ....

Total: ....

NOTES

....

....

ORDER FORM

Date:

Order#:

CUSTOMER DETAILS

Name: ....

Address: ....

Company: ....

Tel. .... **E-mail:** ....

ORDER DETAILS

No	Item(s) Description	QTY.	Price	Total
....	....	....	....	....
....	....	....	....	....
....	....	....	....	....
....	....	....	....	....
....	....	....	....	....
....	....	....	....	....
....	....	....	....	....

SHIPPING DETAILS

Shipping method: ....

Subtotal: ....

....

Shipping cost: ....

Tracking#: ....

Discount: ....

Date shipped: ....

Total: ....

NOTES

....

....

....

ORDER FORM

Date:

Order#:

CUSTOMER DETAILS

Name: ....

Address: ....

Company: ....

Tel. .... **E-mail:** ....

ORDER DETAILS

No	Item(s) Description	QTY.	Price	Total
....	....	....	....	....
....	....	....	....	....
....	....	....	....	....
....	....	....	....	....
....	....	....	....	....
....	....	....	....	....
....	....	....	....	....

SHIPPING DETAILS

Shipping method: ....

....

Tracking#: ....

Date shipped: ....

Subtotal: ....

Shipping cost: ....

Discount: ....

Total: ....

NOTES

....

....

ORDER FORM

Date:

Order#:

CUSTOMER DETAILS

Name: ....

Address: ....

Company: ....

Tel. .... **E-mail:** ....

ORDER DETAILS

No	Item(s) Description	QTY.	Price	Total
....	....	....	....	....
....	....	....	....	....
....	....	....	....	....
....	....	....	....	....
....	....	....	....	....
....	....	....	....	....
....	....	....	....	....

SHIPPING DETAILS

Shipping method: ....

....

Tracking#: ....

Date shipped: ....

Subtotal: ....

Shipping cost: ....

Discount: ....

Total: ....

NOTES

....

....

ORDER FORM

Date:

Order#:

CUSTOMER DETAILS

Name: ....

Address: ....

Company: ....

Tel. .... **E-mail:** ....

ORDER DETAILS

No	Item(s) Description	QTY.	Price	Total
....	....	....	....	....
....	....	....	....	....
....	....	....	....	....
....	....	....	....	....
....	....	....	....	....
....	....	....	....	....
....	....	....	....	....

SHIPPING DETAILS

Shipping method: ....

....

Tracking#: ....

Date shipped: ....

Subtotal: ....

Shipping cost: ....

Discount: ....

Total: ....

NOTES

....

....

ORDER FORM

Date:

Order#:

CUSTOMER DETAILS

Name: ....

Address: ....

Company: ....

Tel. .... E-mail: ....

ORDER DETAILS

No	Item(s) Description	QTY.	Price	Total
....	....	....	....	....
....	....	....	....	....
....	....	....	....	....
....	....	....	....	....
....	....	....	....	....
....	....	....	....	....
....	....	....	....	....

SHIPPING DETAILS

Shipping method: ....

....

Tracking#: ....

Date shipped: ....

Subtotal: ....

Shipping cost: ....

Discount: ....

Total: ....

NOTES

....

....

....

ORDER FORM

Date: ....
Order#: ....

CUSTOMER DETAILS

Name: ....
Address: ....
Company: ....
Tel. .... **E-mail:** ....

ORDER DETAILS

No	Item(s) Description	QTY.	Price	Total
....	....	....	....	....
....	....	....	....	....
....	....	....	....	....
....	....	....	....	....
....	....	....	....	....
....	....	....	....	....
....	....	....	....	....

SHIPPING DETAILS

Shipping method: ....
....

Tracking#: ....

Date shipped: ....

Subtotal: ....

Shipping cost: ....

Discount: ....

Total: ....

NOTES

....
....

ORDER FORM

Date:

Order#:

CUSTOMER DETAILS

Name: ....

Address: ....

Company: ....

Tel. .... E-mail: ....

ORDER DETAILS

No	Item(s) Description	QTY.	Price	Total
....	....	....	....	....
....	....	....	....	....
....	....	....	....	....
....	....	....	....	....
....	....	....	....	....
....	....	....	....	....
....	....	....	....	....

SHIPPING DETAILS

Shipping method: .... Subtotal: ....

.... Shipping cost: ....

Tracking#: .... Discount: ....

Date shipped: .... Total: ....

NOTES

....

....

....

ORDER FORM

Date:

Order#:

CUSTOMER DETAILS

Name: ....

Address: ....

Company: ....

Tel. .... **E-mail:** ....

ORDER DETAILS

No	Item(s) Description	QTY.	Price	Total
....	....	....	....	....
....	....	....	....	....
....	....	....	....	....
....	....	....	....	....
....	....	....	....	....
....	....	....	....	....
....	....	....	....	....

SHIPPING DETAILS

Shipping method: ....

....

Tracking#: ....

Date shipped: ....

Subtotal: ....

Shipping cost: ....

Discount: ....

Total: ....

NOTES

....

....

ORDER FORM

Date: ....

Order#: ....

CUSTOMER DETAILS

Name: ....

Address: ....

Company: ....

Tel. .... E-mail: ....

ORDER DETAILS

No	Item(s) Description	QTY.	Price	Total
......	....	....	....	....
......	....	....	....	....
......	....	....	....	....
......	....	....	....	....
......	....	....	....	....
......	....	....	....	....
......	....	....	....	....

SHIPPING DETAILS

Shipping method: ....

....

Tracking#: ....

Date shipped: ....

Subtotal: ....

Shipping cost: ....

Discount: ....

Total: ....

NOTES

....

....

....

ORDER FORM

Date:

Order#:

CUSTOMER DETAILS

Name: ....

Address: ....

Company: ....

Tel. .... **E-mail:** ....

ORDER DETAILS

No	Item(s) Description	QTY.	Price	Total
....	....	....	....	....
....	....	....	....	....
....	....	....	....	....
....	....	....	....	....
....	....	....	....	....
....	....	....	....	....
....	....	....	....	....

SHIPPING DETAILS

Shipping method: ....

....

Tracking#: ....

Date shipped: ....

Subtotal: ....

Shipping cost: ....

Discount: ....

Total: ....

NOTES

....

....

ORDER FORM

Date:

Order#:

CUSTOMER DETAILS

Name: ....

Address: ....

Company: ....

Tel. .... **E-mail:** ....

ORDER DETAILS

No	Item(s) Description	QTY.	Price	Total
......	....	....	....	....
......	....	....	....	....
......	....	....	....	....
......	....	....	....	....
......	....	....	....	....
......	....	....	....	....
......	....	....	....	....

SHIPPING DETAILS

Shipping method: ....

....

Tracking#: ....

Date shipped: ....

Subtotal: ....

Shipping cost: ....

Discount: ....

Total: ....

NOTES

....

....

....

ORDER FORM

Date:

Order#:

CUSTOMER DETAILS

Name: ....

Address: ....

Company: ....

Tel. .... **E-mail:** ....

ORDER DETAILS

No	Item(s) Description	QTY.	Price	Total
....	....	....	....	....
....	....	....	....	....
....	....	....	....	....
....	....	....	....	....
....	....	....	....	....
....	....	....	....	....
....	....	....	....	....

SHIPPING DETAILS

Shipping method: ....

....

Tracking#: ....

Date shipped: ....

Subtotal: ....

Shipping cost: ....

Discount: ....

Total: ....

NOTES

....

....

....

ORDER FORM

Date:

Order#:

CUSTOMER DETAILS

Name: ....

Address: ....

Company: ....

Tel. .... **E-mail:** ....

ORDER DETAILS

No	Item(s) Description	QTY.	Price	Total
....	....	....	....	....
....	....	....	....	....
....	....	....	....	....
....	....	....	....	....
....	....	....	....	....
....	....	....	....	....
....	....	....	....	....

SHIPPING DETAILS

Shipping method: ....

....

Tracking#: ....

Date shipped: ....

Subtotal: ....

Shipping cost: ....

Discount: ....

Total: ....

NOTES

....

....

....

ORDER FORM

Date:

Order#:

CUSTOMER DETAILS

Name:

Address:

Company:

Tel. .... **E-mail:**

ORDER DETAILS

No	Item(s) Description	QTY.	Price	Total

SHIPPING DETAILS

Shipping method:

Tracking#:

Date shipped:

Subtotal:

Shipping cost:

Discount:

Total:

NOTES

ORDER FORM

Date:

Order#:

CUSTOMER DETAILS

Name: ....

Address: ....

Company: ....

Tel. .... E-mail: ....

ORDER DETAILS

No	Item(s) Description	QTY.	Price	Total
....	....	....	....	....
....	....	....	....	....
....	....	....	....	....
....	....	....	....	....
....	....	....	....	....
....	....	....	....	....
....	....	....	....	....

SHIPPING DETAILS

Shipping method: ....   Subtotal: ....

....   Shipping cost: ....

Tracking#: ....   Discount: ....

Date shipped: ....   Total: ....

NOTES

....

....

....

ORDER FORM

Date: ....

Order#: ....

CUSTOMER DETAILS

Name: ....

Address: ....

Company: ....

Tel. .... E-mail: ....

ORDER DETAILS

No	Item(s) Description	QTY.	Price	Total
....	....	....	....	....
....	....	....	....	....
....	....	....	....	....
....	....	....	....	....
....	....	....	....	....
....	....	....	....	....
....	....	....	....	....

SHIPPING DETAILS

Shipping method: ....

....

Tracking#: ....

Date shipped: ....

Subtotal: ....

Shipping cost: ....

Discount: ....

Total: ....

NOTES

....

....

ORDER FORM

Date:

Order#:

CUSTOMER DETAILS

Name: ....

Address: ....

Company: ....

Tel. .... **E-mail:** ....

ORDER DETAILS

No	Item(s) Description	QTY.	Price	Total

SHIPPING DETAILS

Shipping method: ....

Subtotal: ....

....

Shipping cost: ....

Tracking#: ....

Discount: ....

Date shipped: ....

Total: ....

NOTES

....

....

....

ORDER FORM

Date: ....

Order#: ....

CUSTOMER DETAILS

Name: ....

Address: ....

Company: ....

Tel. .... **E-mail:** ....

ORDER DETAILS

No	Item(s) Description	QTY.	Price	Total
....	....	....	....	....
....	....	....	....	....
....	....	....	....	....
....	....	....	....	....
....	....	....	....	....
....	....	....	....	....
....	....	....	....	....

SHIPPING DETAILS

Shipping method: ....

....

Tracking#: ....

Date shipped: ....

Subtotal: ....

Shipping cost: ....

Discount: ....

Total: ....

NOTES

....

....

ORDER FORM

Date:

Order#:

CUSTOMER DETAILS

Name: ....

Address: ....

Company: ....

Tel. .... **E-mail:** ....

ORDER DETAILS

No	Item(s) Description	QTY.	Price	Total

SHIPPING DETAILS

Shipping method: ....

Subtotal: ....

....

Shipping cost: ....

Tracking#: ....

Discount: ....

Date shipped: ....

Total: ....

NOTES

....

....

....

ORDER FORM

Date: ....

Order#: ....

CUSTOMER DETAILS

Name: ....

Address: ....

Company: ....

Tel. .... **E-mail:** ....

ORDER DETAILS

No	Item(s) Description	QTY.	Price	Total
....	....	....	....	....
....	....	....	....	....
....	....	....	....	....
....	....	....	....	....
....	....	....	....	....
....	....	....	....	....
....	....	....	....	....

SHIPPING DETAILS

Shipping method: ....

....

Tracking#: ....

Date shipped: ....

Subtotal: ....

Shipping cost: ....

Discount: ....

Total: ....

NOTES

....

....

....

ORDER FORM

Date:

Order#:

CUSTOMER DETAILS

Name: ....

Address: ....

Company: ....

Tel. .... E-mail: ....

ORDER DETAILS

No	Item(s) Description	QTY.	Price	Total
....	....	....	....	....
....	....	....	....	....
....	....	....	....	....
....	....	....	....	....
....	....	....	....	....
....	....	....	....	....
....	....	....	....	....

SHIPPING DETAILS

Shipping method: ....

....

Tracking#: ....

Date shipped: ....

Subtotal: ....

Shipping cost: ....

Discount: ....

Total: ....

NOTES

....

....

....

ORDER FORM

Date:

Order#:

CUSTOMER DETAILS

Name: ....

Address: ....

Company: ....

Tel. .... E-mail: ....

ORDER DETAILS

No	Item(s) Description	QTY.	Price	Total
....	....	....	....	....
....	....	....	....	....
....	....	....	....	....
....	....	....	....	....
....	....	....	....	....
....	....	....	....	....
....	....	....	....	....

SHIPPING DETAILS

Shipping method: ....

....

Tracking#: ....

Date shipped: ....

Subtotal: ....

Shipping cost: ....

Discount: ....

Total: ....

NOTES

....

....

....

ORDER FORM

Date:

Order#:

CUSTOMER DETAILS

Name: ....

Address: ....

Company: ....

Tel. .... E-mail: ....

ORDER DETAILS

No	Item(s) Description	QTY.	Price	Total
......	....	....	....	....
......	....	....	....	....
......	....	....	....	....
......	....	....	....	....
......	....	....	....	....
......	....	....	....	....
......	....	....	....	....

SHIPPING DETAILS

Shipping method: ....

....

Tracking#: ....

Date shipped: ....

Subtotal: ....

Shipping cost: ....

Discount: ....

Total: ....

NOTES

....

....

....

ORDER FORM

Date: ....

Order#: ....

CUSTOMER DETAILS

Name: ....

Address: ....

Company: ....

Tel. .... E-mail: ....

ORDER DETAILS

No	Item(s) Description	QTY.	Price	Total
....	....	....	....	....
....	....	....	....	....
....	....	....	....	....
....	....	....	....	....
....	....	....	....	....
....	....	....	....	....
....	....	....	....	....

SHIPPING DETAILS

Shipping method: .... Subtotal: ....

.... Shipping cost: ....

Tracking#: .... Discount: ....

Date shipped: .... Total: ....

NOTES

....

....

....

ORDER FORM

Date:

Order#:

CUSTOMER DETAILS

Name: ....

Address: ....

Company: ....

Tel. .... **E-mail:** ....

ORDER DETAILS

No	Item(s) Description	QTY.	Price	Total
....	....	....	....	....
....	....	....	....	....
....	....	....	....	....
....	....	....	....	....
....	....	....	....	....
....	....	....	....	....
....	....	....	....	....

SHIPPING DETAILS

Shipping method: ....

....

Tracking#: ....

Date shipped: ....

Subtotal: ....

Shipping cost: ....

Discount: ....

Total: ....

NOTES

....

....

ORDER FORM

Date:

Order#:

CUSTOMER DETAILS

Name: ....

Address: ....

Company: ....

Tel. .... **E-mail:** ....

ORDER DETAILS

No	Item(s) Description	QTY.	Price	Total
....	....	....	....	....
....	....	....	....	....
....	....	....	....	....
....	....	....	....	....
....	....	....	....	....
....	....	....	....	....
....	....	....	....	....

SHIPPING DETAILS

Shipping method: ....   **Subtotal:** ....

....   **Shipping cost:** ....

Tracking#: ....   **Discount:** ....

Date shipped: ....   **Total:** ....

NOTES

....

....

ORDER FORM

Date:

Order#:

CUSTOMER DETAILS

Name: ....

Address: ....

Company: ....

Tel. .... E-mail: ....

ORDER DETAILS

No	Item(s) Description	QTY.	Price	Total
....	....	....	....	....
....	....	....	....	....
....	....	....	....	....
....	....	....	....	....
....	....	....	....	....
....	....	....	....	....
....	....	....	....	....

SHIPPING DETAILS

Shipping method: ....

....

Tracking#: ....

Date shipped: ....

Subtotal: ....

Shipping cost: ....

Discount: ....

Total: ....

NOTES

....

....

ORDER FORM

Date:

Order#:

CUSTOMER DETAILS

Name: ....

Address: ....

Company: ....

Tel. .... **E-mail:** ....

ORDER DETAILS

No	Item(s) Description	QTY.	Price	Total
....	....	....	....	....
....	....	....	....	....
....	....	....	....	....
....	....	....	....	....
....	....	....	....	....
....	....	....	....	....
....	....	....	....	....

SHIPPING DETAILS

Shipping method: ....

....

Tracking#: ....

Date shipped: ....

Subtotal: ....

Shipping cost: ....

Discount: ....

Total: ....

NOTES

....

....

ORDER FORM

Date:

Order#:

CUSTOMER DETAILS

Name: ....

Address: ....

Company: ....

Tel. .... E-mail: ....

ORDER DETAILS

No	Item(s) Description	QTY.	Price	Total
....	....	....	....	....
....	....	....	....	....
....	....	....	....	....
....	....	....	....	....
....	....	....	....	....
....	....	....	....	....
....	....	....	....	....

SHIPPING DETAILS

Shipping method: ....

....

Tracking#: ....

Date shipped: ....

Subtotal: ....

Shipping cost: ....

Discount: ....

Total: ....

NOTES

....

....

....

ORDER FORM

Date:

Order#:

CUSTOMER DETAILS

Name: ....

Address: ....

Company: ....

Tel. .... E-mail: ....

ORDER DETAILS

No	Item(s) Description	QTY.	Price	Total
....	....	....	....	....
....	....	....	....	....
....	....	....	....	....
....	....	....	....	....
....	....	....	....	....
....	....	....	....	....
....	....	....	....	....

SHIPPING DETAILS

Shipping method: ....

....

Tracking#: ....

Date shipped: ....

Subtotal: ....

Shipping cost: ....

Discount: ....

Total: ....

NOTES

....

....

ORDER FORM

Date:
Order#:

CUSTOMER DETAILS

Name: ....
Address: ....
Company: ....
Tel. .... E-mail: ....

ORDER DETAILS

No	Item(s) Description	QTY.	Price	Total
....	....	....	....	....
....	....	....	....	....
....	....	....	....	....
....	....	....	....	....
....	....	....	....	....
....	....	....	....	....
....	....	....	....	....

SHIPPING DETAILS

Shipping method: ....
....

Tracking#: ....

Date shipped: ....

Subtotal: ....

Shipping cost: ....

Discount: ....

Total: ....

NOTES

....
....

ORDER FORM

Date: ....

Order#: ....

CUSTOMER DETAILS

Name: ....

Address: ....

Company: ....

Tel. .... **E-mail:** ....

ORDER DETAILS

No	Item(s) Description	QTY.	Price	Total
....	....	....	....	....
....	....	....	....	....
....	....	....	....	....
....	....	....	....	....
....	....	....	....	....
....	....	....	....	....
....	....	....	....	....

SHIPPING DETAILS

Shipping method: ....

....

Tracking#: ....

Date shipped: ....

Subtotal: ....

Shipping cost: ....

Discount: ....

Total: ....

NOTES

....

....

ORDER FORM

Date:

Order#:

CUSTOMER DETAILS

Name: ....

Address: ....

Company: ....

Tel. .... E-mail: ....

ORDER DETAILS

No	Item(s) Description	QTY.	Price	Total
....	....	....	....	....
....	....	....	....	....
....	....	....	....	....
....	....	....	....	....
....	....	....	....	....
....	....	....	....	....
....	....	....	....	....

SHIPPING DETAILS

Shipping method: .... Subtotal: ....

.... Shipping cost: ....

Tracking#: .... Discount: ....

Date shipped: .... Total: ....

NOTES

....

....

ORDER FORM

Date: ....

Order#: ....

CUSTOMER DETAILS

Name: ....

Address: ....

Company: ....

Tel. .... **E-mail:** ....

ORDER DETAILS

No	Item(s) Description	QTY.	Price	Total
....	....	....	....	....
....	....	....	....	....
....	....	....	....	....
....	....	....	....	....
....	....	....	....	....
....	....	....	....	....
....	....	....	....	....

SHIPPING DETAILS

Shipping method: ....

....

Tracking#: ....

Date shipped: ....

Subtotal: ....

Shipping cost: ....

Discount: ....

Total: ....

NOTES

....

....

ORDER FORM

Date:

Order#:

CUSTOMER DETAILS

Name: ....

Address: ....

Company: ....

Tel. .... E-mail: ....

ORDER DETAILS

No	Item(s) Description	QTY.	Price	Total
....	....	....	....	....
....	....	....	....	....
....	....	....	....	....
....	....	....	....	....
....	....	....	....	....
....	....	....	....	....
....	....	....	....	....

SHIPPING DETAILS

Shipping method: ....

....

Tracking#: ....

Date shipped: ....

Subtotal: ....

Shipping cost: ....

Discount: ....

Total: ....

NOTES

....

....

....

ORDER FORM

Date:

Order#:

CUSTOMER DETAILS

Name: ....

Address: ....

Company: ....

Tel. .... **E-mail:** ....

ORDER DETAILS

No	Item(s) Description	QTY.	Price	Total
....	....	....	....	....
....	....	....	....	....
....	....	....	....	....
....	....	....	....	....
....	....	....	....	....
....	....	....	....	....
....	....	....	....	....

SHIPPING DETAILS

Shipping method: ....

....

Tracking#: ....

Date shipped: ....

Subtotal: ....

Shipping cost: ....

Discount: ....

Total: ....

NOTES

....

....

Manufactured by Amazon.ca
Bolton, ON

30743122R00083